Rick and Morty™

THE OFFICIAL COLORING BOOK

SOMETIMES SCIENCE IS MORE ART THAN SCIENCE

INSIGHT EDITIONS
San Rafael • Los Angeles • London

SCHWIFTY

WE'RE HERE
WE'RE SHEER
WE WILL NOT BE
IGNORED
LEGAL

DO NOT
DEVELOP
MY APP

Professor-
Poopybutthole
Ooowee
$\pi = 3.14$
$(y+A) = \frac{2}{3}A$
$c = \pi r^2$

Merry Christmassssss

SSSS
SSSS!!

CLONE BETH
BETH

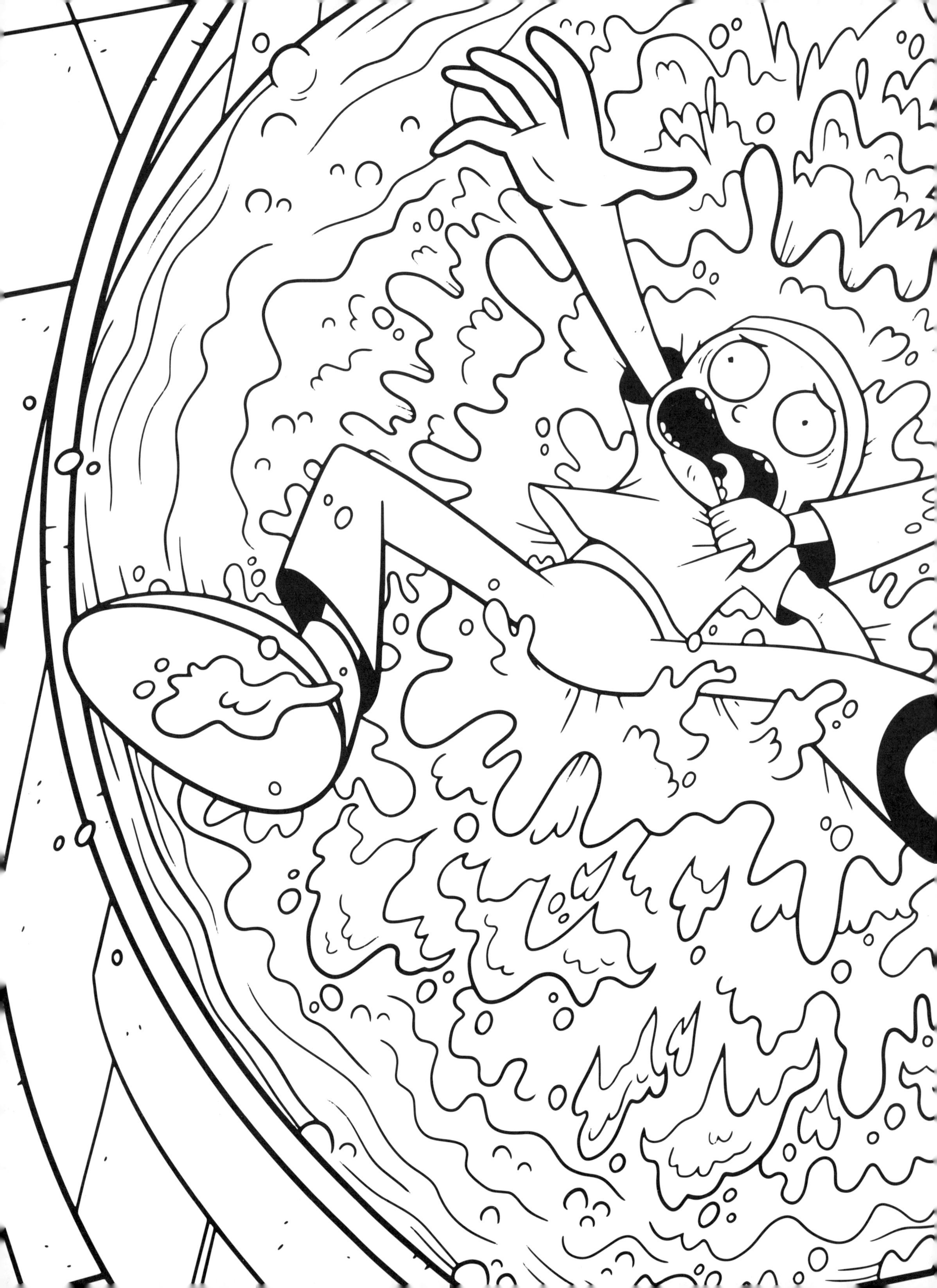

HANDS OFF!

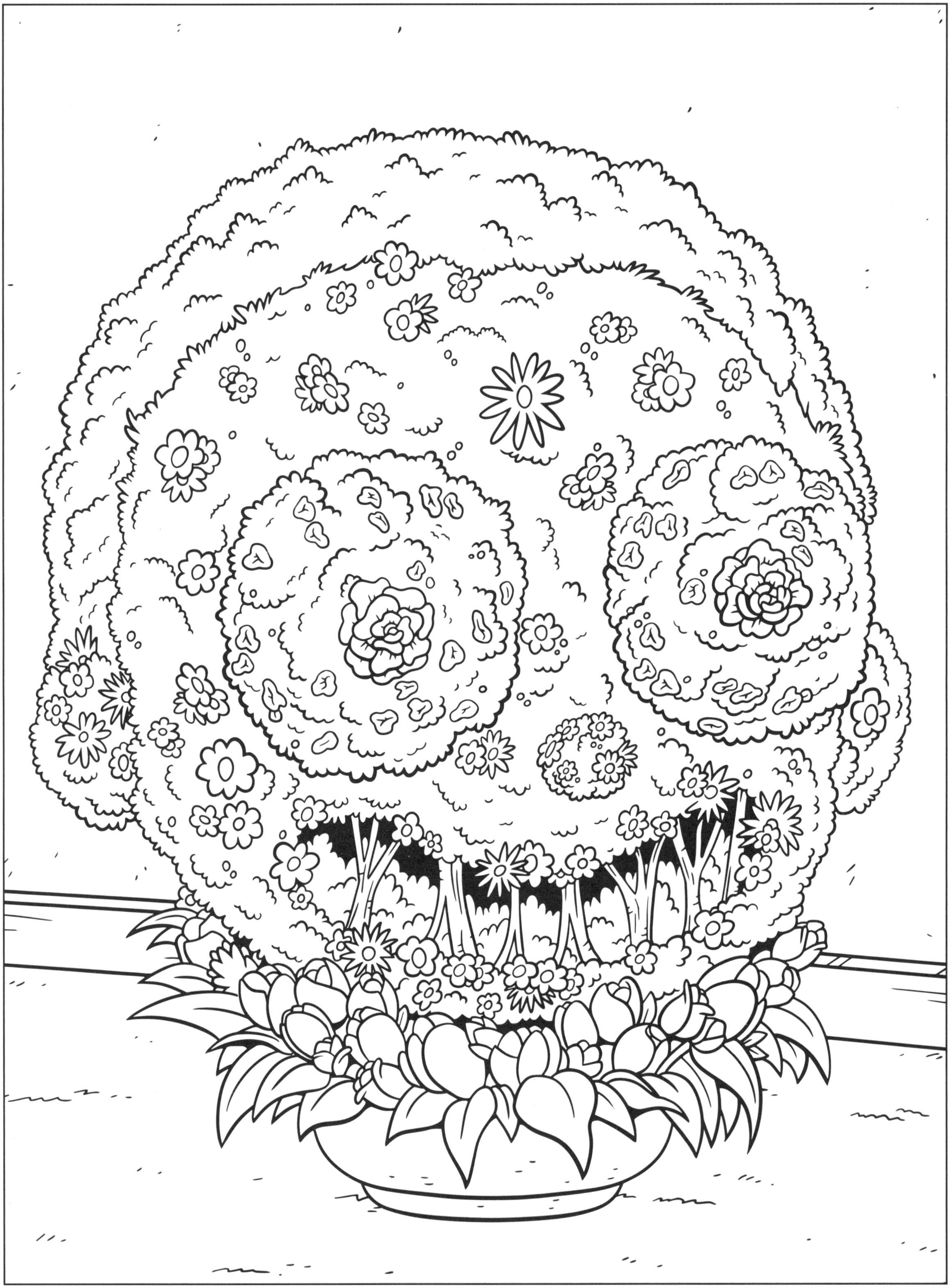

CITADEL
NEWS